6

Len and Anne Frobisher

Heinemann
Halley Court, Jordan Hill, Oxford, OX2 8EJ
a division of Reed Educational and Professional Publishing Ltd
www.myprimary.co.uk

Heinemann is a registered trademark of Reed Educational and Professional Publishing Ltd

ISBN 0 435 20867 5 / 9780435208677 (Pupil Book)
ISBN 0 435 20875 6 / 9780435208752 (Teacher's version)

10 9 8 7 6 5 4
09 08 07 06

Illustrated by Andy Hammond

Cover illustration by Andy Hunt

Typesetting and layout by DP Press Ltd, Sevenoaks, Kent

Printed by Ashford Colour Press Ltd., Gosport, Hants.

Contents

WORD PROBLEMS YEAR 6

Number problems 1

❶ In a golf tournament Julie has rounds of 86 and 95.

What is Julie's total score? **181**

❷ In a gymnastics competition a team has ten members. They each score 8.9 points.

What is the total points score of the team? **89**

❸ A machine makes 37 000 candles each day and packs them into boxes of 100.

How many boxes are packed each day? **370**

❹ A car park has 63 parking places. There are 47 cars in the car park.

How many empty places are there? **16**

❺ Ten judges give a total score of 45 in an ice-skating competition. Each judge awards the same score.

What score did each judge award? **4.5**

❻ There are 100 paper clips in a box and 100 boxes in a carton.

How many paper clips are in one carton? **10 000**

❼

Divide me by 10 and multiply the answer by 100. You will get 32. What am I?

3.2

4

Money problems 1

❶ Mr Hobson buys a car for himself for £5900 and another for his wife for £3800. What is the total cost of the two cars?
£9700

❷ A newsagent sells 25 copies of a magazine. Each copy is £3.60. What is the total amount of money that the newsagent receives? **£900**

❸ Mr and Mrs Reed book a round the world holiday. The total cost is £9200. They pay a deposit of £1700. How much is left for them to pay? **£7500**

❹ The normal price for a TV is £500. In the sale it is reduced by 25%. By how much is the TV reduced?
£125

❺ Nigel's mum buys a microwave for £84.90 and a vacuum cleaner for £37.50 from a catalogue. How much does she pay when she collects them? **£122.40**

❻ Mr Grey buys 25 swing ball sets to sell in his shop. He pays a total of £440. How much does he pay for each swing ball set? **£17.60**

❼

I am between £6 and £9.
I am a multiple of 50p.
I divide exactly by 2 and by 3.

What am I?

£7.50

Number problems 2

1 Helen wants 42 balloons for a party. Each packet has 6 balloons.

How many packets does she need to buy? **7**

2 In two high board dives Sean was awarded a total of 10 points. In his first dive Ashley scored 5.2 points.

How many points does Ashley need to equal Sean's total? **4.8**

3 Bradchester's football ground has a capacity of 7495 spectators. In six successive home games it plays in front of a full ground.

What is the total number of spectators who watch the six games? **44 970**

4 Mrs Brian counts 33 children on to a bus for a school trip. There are 76 more still to come.

How many children are going on the school trip? **109**

5 Mr Evans, a baker, makes 72 muffins. He puts them on trays 8 muffins to each tray.

How many trays does he use? **9**

6 In an RSPCA kennels there are 82 stray dogs. Shortly after Christmas another 18 strays are brought in.

How many stray dogs are in the kennels then? **100**

7 *I am a square number.*
I am less than 80.
I am a multiple of 9.
What am I?

36

Number problems 3

fractions;
multiples of 50 total 1000;
× facts

1 There are 850 passengers waiting for trains. Another 150 join them.
What is the total number waiting for trains? **1000**

2 An airport has seven stands for planes. Each stand can take eight planes.
What is the total number of planes on the stands when they are all full? **56**

3 Pasta King makes ten pizzas. Each pizza is cut into six pieces. They sell three whole pizzas and 5 single pieces.

How many pizzas are left as a mixed number? **$6\frac{1}{6}$**

4 In every pack there are six packets of crisps. Each packet weighs 25 g. Philippa buys eight packs for a party.

How many packets of crisps does Philippa buy? **48**

5 On the first day of a two-day Steam Fair 350 balloons are launched in a distance competition. On the second day another 650 are let go.
Altogether how many balloons are launched? **1000**

6 A cafe makes six apple pies. Each apple pie is cut into eighths. The cafe sells $4\frac{3}{4}$ pies.
How many eighths are left? **10**

7

*I am a square number.
I am the sum of three odd numbers between 20 and 30.*

What am I?

81

7

Number problems 4

---

1 At Glenn Primary School 3 in every 5 children are girls.

What percentage of the children are girls? **60%**

2 There are 15 people in an adult swimming lesson. For every 2 men there are 3 women.

How many are men? **6**
How many are women? **9**

---

3 Watley Cricket Club has won 50% of their 20 matches and drawn 10%.

How many matches has Watney CC lost? **8**

4 A box contains 20 golf balls. One in every five balls are found to be faulty.

How many golf balls in the box are faulty? **4**

---

5 Three-tenths of a case of oranges are thrown away as they are bad.
What percentage of the oranges are OK? **70%**

---

6 A maths test had 20 questions. Flo got 85% correct.
How many questions did Flo get wrong? **3**

7

I have three factors.
The sum of my factors is 7.

What am I?

4

Number problems 5

❶ A car transporter with a trailer always carries 14 cars. In two years it makes 1000 deliveries. How many cars does it deliver in the two years? **14 000**

❷ Tim plays a game of 'Score 4 or more' with Stan. They take turns to throw a six-sided dice. A point is awarded if they roll 4 or more.

What is the probability that Tim will score a point when he rolls the dice? $\frac{1}{2}$

❸ Holly keeps fish. She has seven large tanks. In each tank there are 28 fish.

Altogether how many fish does Holly have? **196**

❹ Robert tosses a fair coin five times. Each time it lands 'head'.

What is the probability that next time he tosses the coin it will land 'head'? $\frac{1}{2}$

❺ A school has seven classes. Two classes have 27 children, two classes have 30 children and three classes have 25 children.

What is the mean and range of the number of children in the seven classes? **27, 5**

❻ In one day a machine produces 137 000 vitamin tablets and puts them in jars of 1000.

1000 VITAMIN TABLETS

How many jars does it fill in the one day? **137**

❼

I am more than 70. I am the sum of three consecutive numbers. The difference between my two digits is 3.

What am I?

96

Ticket prices

Adults (16-59) £9.00
(£9.50 1 July-30 September)

Children (5-15) £5.00

Senior Citizens (60+) £7.00
(£7.50 1 July-30 September)

To book a ticket call
0870 5000 600

50p booking fee
per ticket

THE LONDON EYE

ENTRANCE

Operating hours

1 Jan-25 May:	10:00-19:00
26 May-9 Sept:	10:00-22:00
10 Sept-30 Sept:	10:00-20:00
1 Oct-31 Dec:	10:00-19:00

Information:

London Eye has
32 capsules

Each capsule
holds 25 people

Full wheelchair
access

1 Mr and Mrs Upton took their family, Emma (17), Vince (14), Joanne (12) and the children's grandmother (63) and grandfather (62) to ride on the London Eye during the summer holidays. They had booked their tickets two weeks before they went.
What was the total cost for the seven of them? **£57**

2 How much would the Upton family have saved had they gone in May instead of the summer holidays? **£2**

3 The Upton family travelled from Newcastle by train. They got the 07:30 train which was due to arrive in King's Cross, London at 10:50. It arrived 17 minutes late.
How long did the journey take? **3 hr 37 min**

4 The London Eye operates every day of the year.
What is the total number of hours it is operating in one year? **3627 hr**

5 How many people are on the London Eye when it is full? **800**

6 A ride on the Eye takes a gently paced half an hour. The ride moves at the same speed and never stops moving until it closes at the end of the day.
How many full turns did it make on 15th September? **20**

7 If there is a metal rope from the centre of the Eye to each capsule, what is the angle between each rope? **11.25°**

8 The average weight of a man is 73.5 kg and a woman 61.3 kg. What is the approximate total weight in a capsule which contains 10 men and 10 women? **1348 kg**

9 The Eye is 135 metres high. A double-decker bus is 5 metres high. How many times higher is the Eye than a double-decker bus? **27**

10 It is predicted that 2 million visitors will ride on the Eye every year for the next five years. If the actual number is only 90% of the prediction how many will ride on the Eye in the next five years? **9 million**

Measures problems 1

1 Adam tried to triple jump for the first time. He hopped 2.7 m, stepped 1.8 m and jumped 2.9 metres.

How long was his triple jump? **7.4 m**

2 An average 10-year-old boy weighs 36 kg. This is 10 times the average weight of a newly born boy.

What is the average weight of a newly born boy? **3.6 kg**

---

3 An A4 sheet of paper is 21 cm wide and 29.7 cm long.

What is the perimeter of a piece of A4 paper? **101.4 cm**

---

4 Adele buys an electric radiator. It is 25 cm tall and 60 cm wide.

What is the total surface area of the radiator? **3000 cm²**

5 Charlotte opens a full bottle of 2.5 litres of lemonade. She pours out two glasses with 200 mL in each glass.

How much lemonade is left in the bottle? **2100 mL**

---

6 Steve flies from London to Sydney. The total time for the journey was 45 hours. The plane stops at three airports to refuel for a total of 17 hours.
For how long was Steve actually flying? **28 hr**

7
I am the sum of four consecutive numbers. The four numbers are between 16 and 23. The first and last numbers are multiples of 3.

What am I?

78

Length problems 1

percentages;
miles/km;
facts/pv to +/–;
×10/100

1 In 1991 the world record for the long jump, set by Mike Powell, was 8.95 m. A fully sized python is 20% longer than this.
How long is a fully sized python? **10.74 m**

2 In 1930 a man dived into the sea using only air to a depth of 105 m. Thirty years later a man in a bathyscaphe went to 100 times this depth.
How many kilometres deep did the bathyscaphe go? **10.5 km**

3 The longest Olympic event is the 50 km road walk.

What is the length of the walk in miles to the nearest mile? **31 miles**

4 In the year 2000 the women's javelin record was 67.09 m. The men's record was 98.48 m.
How much longer was the men's than the women's record distance? **31.39 m**

5 The distance from Paris, France to Rome, Italy is 1098 km. The distance from New York, USA to Beijing, China is 10 times this.

How far is it from New York to Beijing? **10980 km**

6 The tallest building in the world used to be the Empire State Building in New York at 381 m. In 2001 the tallest was the CN Tower in Toronto. It is 128 m higher than the Empire State Building.

What is the height of the CN Tower? **509 m**

7

I have only two factors. The difference between the two factors is 16.

What am I?

17

Time problems 1

time zones;
facts/pv to ×/÷;
multiples of 50 total
1000

❶ When people are eating breakfast in New York at 8 a.m. Londoners are having lunch at 1 p.m.

NEW YORK   LONDON

What is the time difference between New York and London?   **5 hr**

---

❷ Beth has a seconds watch. Her brother runs on the spot for 750 seconds and jumps up and down for 250 seconds.

What is the total time on Beth's watch in minutes and seconds?   **16 min 40 sec**

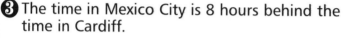

---

❸ The time in Mexico City is 8 hours behind the time in Cardiff.

What day and time is it in Mexico City when it is 3 a.m. on a Tuesday in Cardiff?   **Mon 7pm**

---

❹ Marvin breathes in and out in 1.9 seconds.

How many seconds will it take him to breathe in and out 100 times?   **190 sec**

---

❺ Samantha measures her pulse rate. She finds that her pulse beats 100 times in 90 seconds.

How many seconds is one pulse beat?   **0.9 sec**

❻ Tokyo in Japan is 9 hours ahead of the time in Belfast. It is 08:00 on a Sunday in Tokyo.

What day and time is it in Belfast?   **Sat 23:00**

---

❼

I am the sum of five consecutive numbers. The middle of the five numbers is 15.

What am I?

75

Money problems 2

1 Louise posts a letter and a parcel. The letter costs her £0.85 and the parcel double the cost of the letter.

How much does the parcel cost Louise? **£1.70**

2 Gaby's mum and dad buy the table and four chairs, and the cupboard.

What is the total cost of the table, chairs and cupboard? **£455**

3 The normal price of a car is £12 000. Craig's dad gets a discount of £1200.

What is the percentage discount that Craig's dad gets? **10%**

4 Moira goes with her friends for a party meal at Billy Burgers. It costs her dad £51 for the ten of them.
What is the average cost for each person? **£5.10**

5 Katie's mum withdraws £500 from the bank. She spends £397 of it on a short holiday for the family.
How much of the £500 is left? **£103**

6 The pre-sale price for a camcorder is £650. It is reduced in the sale by 20%.
What is the price of the camcorder in the sale? **£520**

7

I am only divisible by 1 and 37.

What am I?

37

15

Number problems 6

❶ A company employs 3841 workers. It merges with another company that has 1996 employees to form a new company.

How many people are employed by the merged new company? **5837**

❷ Andrea takes part in a gymnastics competition. In her first attempt on the beam she falls and only scores 4.6 points. She scores double this on her second attempt.

How many does Andrea score on her second attempt? **9.2**

❸ At the Autumn Fair Fiona sells cakes. She displays eight plates with eight tarts on each plate.

Altogether how many tarts are on the plates? **64**

❹ The attendance at Birchfield Ladies first football match was 1741. The attendance at the next game increased to 2219.

What was the increase in attendance? **478**

❺ A local council owns houses and flats. There are 8608 people living in houses and 4295 in flats.

What is the total number of people living in houses and flats? **12 903**

❻ Robchester Rugby Club's ground has room for 7157 spectators. There are 2994 seats.

How many spectators stand when the ground is full? **4163**

❼

My greatest factor is 64.

What am I?

64

Number problems 7

1 Jumpers are boxed in sixes. Mr Harvey takes delivery of 43 boxes for his shop.
How many jumpers have been delivered to his shop? **258**

2 In a competition there are 180 hot air balloons. One hour after the time to take off one-tenth of them are still on the ground.
How many are still on the ground? **18**

3 The cost of a packet of Wheatcrunch is £1.25. The number in a packet is increased from 24 to 36 without an increase in the price.
What is the percentage increase in the number of Wheatcrunches in a box? **50%**

4 In an hour, a machine makes 300 000 chocolate drops and puts them into packets of 100.

How many packets are produced in one hour? **3000**

5 In a dance competition Jodie and Thomas score 4.4 points in the Jive and 5.6 points in the Disco.
What is their total score after the two dances? **10**

6 Medallions are made of famous athletes to celebrate the Olympic Games. A machine makes 1 million every day. They are packed in boxes of 1000.
How many boxes are packed every day? **1000**

7 *The sum of my four prime factors is 17.*

What am I?

210

17

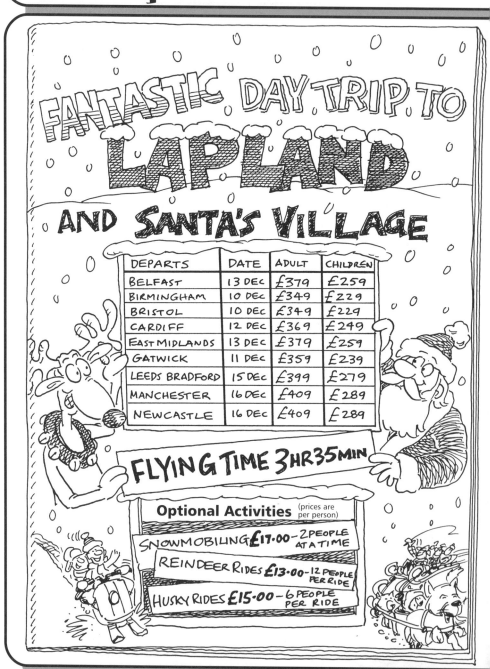

FANTASTIC DAY TRIP TO LAPLAND

AND SANTA'S VILLAGE

DEPARTS	DATE	ADULT	CHILDREN
BELFAST	13 DEC	£379	£259
BIRMINGHAM	10 DEC	£349	£229
BRISTOL	10 DEC	£349	£229
CARDIFF	12 DEC	£369	£249
EAST MIDLANDS	13 DEC	£379	£259
GATWICK	11 DEC	£359	£239
LEEDS BRADFORD	15 DEC	£399	£279
MANCHESTER	16 DEC	£409	£289
NEWCASTLE	16 DEC	£409	£289

FLYING TIME 3HR 35MIN

Optional Activities (prices are per person)

SNOWMOBILING £17.00 – 2 PEOPLE AT A TIME

REINDEER RIDES £13.00 – 12 PEOPLE PER RIDE

HUSKY RIDES £15.00 – 6 PEOPLE PER RIDE

1 Mr and Mrs Davies live between Bristol and Cardiff. They want to take their three children to Lapland.
How much will it cost them to go from Cardiff? **£1485**
How much cheaper would it be for them to go from Bristol? **£100**

2 It takes the Davies family 1 hr 15 min to get to Cardiff Airport. They should arrive 2 hours before the 07:05 flight.
At what time should they leave home? **03:50**

3 At what time is the 07:05 flight from Cardiff due to land in Lapland? **10:40**

4 The distance from Mr and Mrs Davies' home to Cardiff airport is 80 km. From Cardiff to Santa's Village is 2370 km.
How far will the Davies family have travelled when they arrive home? **4900 km**

5 When the Davies family travel there are 3 children in every 5 people on board the plane. Altogether there are 135 passengers.
How many children are on the plane? **81**

6 On the flight from Belfast there are 58 adults and 97 children, and 10 crew. What is the total number of people on the plane? **165**

7 Altogether a total of 1251 people travel to Lapland on the advertised flights.
What is the average number of passengers per airport? **139**

8 When they arrive in Lapland Mr Davies and two of the children go on a snowmobile and the whole family go on a reindeer sleigh ride. Altogether how much does it cost them? **£116**

9 There are ten sleighs each pulled by eight huskies at the Santa Claus Village. How many huskies are there altogether? **80**

10 On the East Midlands trip 79 people wish to go on a reindeer ride. How many journeys will the sleighs make? **7**

11 A large group of 36 children and 20 adults book from Manchester. They get a reduction of 15% off the total cost.
How much does the group pay? **£15 796.40**

12 Plan and cost a visit to Lapland for your family.

19

Number problems 8

1 Jamie and his friends give out leaflets advertising a rock concert. On Monday they give out 6000, on Tuesday 8000 and on Wednesday 5000. Altogether how many leaflets did they give out? **19 000**

2 In the first hour of a sale 93 people enter a shop. Of these, 78 buy an item in the sale.

How many do not buy an item? **15**

3 In South Dakota, USA, on 22nd January 1943 the temperature rose from –20°C to 7°C in two minutes.
By how many degrees did the temperature rise in the two minutes? **27°C**

4 There were 7200 tickets sold for an open air concert. It rained heavily on the night and only 6700 people attended.
How many people with tickets did not attend the concert? **500**

5 Year 5 sell 72 tickets for a combined Year 5 and Year 6 disco. Year 6 sell 89 tickets.

YEAR 5&6
DISCO
DECEMBER 12
IN THE
SCHOOL HALL 36
ADMIT ONE

Altogether how many tickets do they sell? **161**

6 At 11 p.m. the temperature at a school is –1°C. Seven hours later it has dropped by 4°C.

What is the temperature at 6 a.m? **–5°C**

7
If you double me and subtract 1000 from the answer you get 4000. What am I?

2500

Money problems 3

percentages;
multiples of 50 total 1000;
pairs total 100;
facts/pv to ×/÷

1 The normal price of the lawnmower is £600.
What is the sale price of the lawn mower? **£400**

2 For her 18th birthday Millie's mum and dad buy her the ring and chain.
What is the total cost of the two items? **£100**

3 A china cup and saucer cost £7.60. Nel's mum buys eight cups and saucers.

What is the total cost of the eight cups and saucers? **£60.80**

4 Brad's aunt is getting married. His mum and dad spend £100 on two presents. They buy her the cutlery set.

How much do they spend on the kettle? **£24.50**

5 A pack of ten monster ice lollies costs £4.30.
What is the cost of one monster ice lolly? **43p**

6 Tino's dad buys the motor car. He pays by credit card.
How much cash does he get back? **£1750**

7

I am a square number between 100 and 200. The sum of my first and last digits is 2 less than my middle digit.

What am I?

196

21

Number problems 9

1 A golf club has 500 members. Of these, 95% are adults.

How many members are children? **25**

2 Five judges in a speaking competition each give Matthew 4.6 marks out of 5.

What is Matthew's total score? **23**

3 Euan went on holiday for six days. He left lights on in the house and used 82.2 units of electricity.

How many units of electricity were used on each of the six days? **13.7**

4 The earth's atmosphere is 78% nitrogen and 21% oxygen.

What percentage of the atmosphere is made up of other gases? **1%**

5 Ancient Egyptians made four mud bricks using a wooden frame.

How many times would they have used the frame to make 748 bricks? **187**

6 Amanda throws three darts. She scores a total of 57. All three darts land in the same number.

What number did the darts land in? **19**

7

I am the smallest number that is divisible by 5, 6 and 9.

What am I?

90

(22)

Number problems 10

fractions;
+/– 2D numbers;
decimals total 10;
÷1000

1 A garden centre has 36 rose trees for sale. Another 48 rose trees are delivered and put out for sale.
How many rose trees are for sale after the delivery? **84**

2 A design in the floor of a Spanish house is made up of regular decagons, 10-sided polygons. Each angle is one-tenth of 1440°.
How many degrees is each angle in a regular decagon? **144°**

3 A supermarket puts 95 Easter eggs on a shelf. They sell 58 of them within 30 minutes of opening.

How many Easter eggs are left on the shelf? **37**

4 The ship carries 1000 cars. In one year the ship transports 8000 cars from Japan to Europe.

How many journeys does the ship make from Japan to Europe? **8**

5 A publisher prints 3000 copies of a book. Two-fifths of the books have to be reprinted as they have pages missing.

How many books have to be reprinted? **1200**

6 In a funny faces competition Mel scores 5.8 with her first funny face and 4.2 with her next.

How many did she score altogether? **10**

7

I am a two-digit number between 10 and 40. I am the sum of all my divisors.

What am I?

28

Measure problems 2

angles;
halve decimals;
decimals total 1;
× 1000; facts to ÷

❶ A spider in Papua New Guinea makes webs which are 1.5 m across.

How many centimetres across is a web? **150 cm**

❷ The rhinoceros beetle is 19 cm long, including its horn. Its horn is one-half of its length.

How long is the horn of the rhinoceros beetle? **9.5 cm**

❸ The track in a go-kart race is triangular. The triangle has angles of 60° and 85°.
What is the size of the third angle of the triangle? **35°**

❹ Simon buys 0.7 kg of strawberries. He gives half of them to his brother.

How many grams of strawberries does Simon have left? **350 g**

❺ A three-toed sloth spends 0.75 of a day hanging upside down.

What fraction of a day does it spend the right way up? $\frac{1}{4}$

❻ A bottle of Jamult holds 65 ml. They are sold in packs of seven. They are delivered to supermarkets in crates of 1000 packs.

How many litres of Jamult is in each crate? **455 L**

❼

I am half-way between two consecutive numbers. The product of the two numbers is 650.

What am I?

25.5

Teachers' Notes

Contents

Introduction

The Pupils' books

Word Problems, a series of four books, one for each of the years 3 to 6, helps develop children's ability to solve number problems in a variety of contexts. Each page of word problems may be used to support numeracy lessons taught earlier in a week or for homework. The books provide weekly practice of word problems, as described in the National Numeracy Strategy (NNS) *Framework* and are designed to match the weekly structure within the NNS 'sample medium-term plans'. The style of questions reflects the examples that appear in the National Curriculum tests.

The books contain two types of page:

Topic pages: Each page has six word problems which are devoted solely to one Topic (Number; Money; Time; Length; Weight; Capacity and Measures). The overall mathematical content of all the Topic pages is listed on page iii. The mathematical content of the word problems on each page is listed in the lozenge at the top of the page.

Question 7 on each Topic page is a number puzzle which gives children practice in Reasoning with Number using a variety of number properties. These questions are similar to those in the *Framework* and the National Curriculum tests.

Review pages look back at the mathematical content of previous Topic pages. Some Review pages are double page spreads, with the left page having a scene with information that is required to answer questions and the right page asking questions about the scene.

Illustrations are used to tune children in to the 'real life' context of the word problem. Each is part of the problem and it is important that children look at the illustrations closely; they may contain information that is also in the word problem itself. On some occasions an illustration will contain information that is not in the text of the word problem, but is essential in order to solve the problem.

Answers to word problems are printed in red at the side of each question in the pupils' pages of the Teachers' notes.

Helping children solve word problems

Here are some suggestions for helping children develop a strategy for solving word problems.

- Make sure children read a question carefully and not merely search for key words such as 'altogether' which they think, sometimes incorrectly, tell them what to do with the numbers.

- Encourage children to close their eyes and picture the context of a problem and any actions that are performed with/on 'objects' in the context.

- Allow children to talk with other children about a problem and to ask themselves:
  - 'What do I have to find out?'
  - 'What do I know that will help me find out?'
  - 'What do I have to do with what I know to find out?'

It is also important as part of a word problem solving strategy that children develop:

- the skill of recognising information that is helpful and that which is not helpful when trying to solve a word problem.

- the ability to choose and use appropriate operations to solve word problems.

These can only develop with experience of solving many word problems over a long period of time.

Calculators

In Year 6 of the NNS *Framework* children are expected to decide when it is appropriate to calculate mentally, with written support or to use a calculator. You will need to discuss with your children which of the methods they feel are suitable for different word problems and have calculators available when they feel they need to use them. However, it is important that you encourage them to try to solve word problems either mentally or with written support as much as possible. This will differ from child to child.

Teaching plans

To enable you to integrate *Word Problems* into your medium-term teaching plans pages vi to iv show the relationship between the Topics in *Word Problems* and the Sample Medium-term plans suggested by the NNS. Pages vii and viii show how the Topics in *Word Problems* relate to Mathematics in the National Curriculum in Wales Programme of Study and also the Programme of Study for Northern Ireland.

Summary of mathematical content

page	topic	Mathematical content
4	Number 1	+/− 2D numbers; ×/÷ 10 and 100
5	Money 1	percentages, use facts/pv to +/− ; ×/÷ 25
6	Number 2	pairs total 100; decimals total 10; ThHTU×U; ÷ facts
7	Number 3	fractions; multiples of 50 total 1000; × facts;
8	Number 4	percentages; ratio; proportion
9	Number 5	probability; mean; range; TU×U; ×/÷1000
10–11	**Review 1**	**review of previous content**
12	Measures 1	+/− 2D numbers; facts/pv to ×/÷;
13	Length 1	percentages; miles/km; facts/pv to +/−; ×10/100
14	Time 1	time zones; facts/pv to ×/÷; multiples of 50 total 1000
15	Money 2	percentages; +/− near multiples of 100; facts/pv to ×/÷
16	Number 6	double decimals; +/− near multiples of 100; ThHTU+/−ThHTU; × facts
17	Number 7	percentages; decimals total 10; TU×U; ÷10/100/1000
18–19	**Review 2**	**review of previous content**
20	Number 8	-ve numbers; facts/pv to +/−; +/− 2D numbers
21	Money 3	percentages; multiples of 50 total 1000; pairs total 100; facts/pv to ×/÷;
22	Number 9	percentages; facts/pv to ×; TU/HTU÷U; TU.t ÷U
23	Number 10	fractions; +/− 2D numbers; decimals total 10; ÷1000
24	Measures 2	angles; halve decimals; decimals total 1; × 1000; facts to ÷
25	**Review 3**	**review of previous content**
26	Weight 1	percentages; g/kg to oz/lb; TU×U; facts/pv to ÷
27	Measures 3	decimals total 0.1; ×/÷ 10; ÷ decimals by 2
28	Money 4	percentages; +/− large numbers; pairs total 100; multiples of 50 total 1000
29	Number 11	+/− decimals; +/− large numbers; facts/pv to ×/÷
30	Number 12	percentages; four operations with large numbers; -ve numbers
31	Number 13	multi-step problems
32–33	**Review 4**	**review of previous content**
34	Number 14	percentages; +/− large numbers; TU/U.t×U
35	Money 5	+/− decimals; HTU×TU; £.p ÷U; facts/pv to ×/÷
36	Number 15	double decimals; +/− large numbers; facts/pv to ÷; HTU ×/÷TU
37	Number 16	percentages; ratio; halves of decimals; ×/÷10
38	Number 17	percentages; proportion; +/− 2D numbers; ×/÷100
39	Number 18	proportion; +/− large numbers; facts/pv to ×; ×/÷1000
40–41	**Review 5**	**review of previous content**
42	Capacity 1	percentages; ratio; gals to litres; ×/÷10
43	Measures 4	four operations
44	Number 19	+/− large numbers; ×/÷1000; U.t×U
45	Money 6	double decimals; percentages; facts to +/−; +/ large numbers;
46	Number 20	halves of decimals; percentages; +/− large numbers; facts/pv to ×/÷
47	Number 21	multi-step problems
48	**Review 6**	**review of previous content**

Word Problems and the National Numeracy Strategy
Sample medium-term plans

AUTUMN			
Sample medium-term plans		**Word Problems**	
Unit	**Topic**	**Pages**	**Topic**
1	Place value; ordering; rounding Using a calculator	4	Number 1
2–3	Understanding × and ÷ Mental calculation strategies (× and ÷) Paper and pencil procedures (× and ÷) Money and 'real life' problems Making decisions; checking results including using a calculator	5–6	Money 1 Number 2
4-5	Fractions, decimals and percentages Ratio and proportion	7–8	Number 3 Number 4
6	Handling data Using a calculator	9	Number 5
7	**Assess and review**	**10–11**	**Review 1**
8–10	Shape and space Reasoning about shapes Measures, including problems	12–14	Measures 1 Length 1 Time 1
11	Mental calculation strategies (+ and −) Pencil and paper procedures (+ and −) Money and 'real life' problems Making decisions, checking results, including using a calculator	15–16	Money 2 Number 6
12	Properties of numbers Reasoning about numbers	17	Number 7
13	**Assess and review**	**18–19**	**Review 2**

SPRING			
Sample medium-term plans		*Word Problems*	
Unit	Topic	Pages	Topic
1	Place value; ordering; rounding Using a calculator	20	Number 8
2–3	Understanding $\times$ and $\div$ Mental calculation strategies ($\times$ and $\div$) Paper and pencil procedures ($\times$ and $\div$) Money and 'real life' problems Making decisions and checking results including using a calculator	21 22	Money 3 Number 9
4	Fractions, decimals and percentages Using a calculator	23	Number 10
5	Shape and space Reasoning about shapes	24	Measures 2
6	**Assess and review**	**25**	**Review 3**
7–8	Measures including problems Handling data	26 27	Weight 1 Measures 3
9–10	Mental calculation strategies ($+$ and $-$) Pencil and paper procedures ($+$ and $-$) Money and 'real life' problems Making decisions, checking results, including using a calculator	28 29 30	Money 4 Number 11 Number 12
11	Properties of numbers Reasoning about numbers	31	Number 13
12	**Assess and review**	**32–33**	**Review 4**

SUMMER			
Sample medium-term plans		**Word Problems**	
Unit	Topic	Pages	Topic
1	Place value, ordering, rounding Using a calculator	34	Number 14
2–3	Understanding $\times$ and $\div$ Mental calculation strategies ($\times$ and $\div$) Paper and pencil procedures ($\times$ and $\div$) Money and 'real life' problems Making decisions and checking results including using a calculator	35–36	Money 5 Number 15
4–5	Fractions, decimals and percentages Ratio and proportion	37–38	Number 16 Number 17
6	Handling data Using a calculator	39	Number 18
7	**Assess and review**	**40–41**	**Review 5**
8–10	Shape and space Reasoning about shapes Measures, including problems	42–44	Capacity 1 Measures 4 Number 19
11	Mental calculation strategies ($+$ and $-$) Pencil and paper procedures ($+$ and $-$) Money and 'real life' problems Making decisions, checking results, including using a calculator	45–46	Money 6 Number 20
12	Properties of numbers Reasoning about numbers	47	Number 21
13	**Assess and review**	**48**	**Review 6**

Word Problems and the National Curriculum in Wales

Using and Applying Mathematics
U1. Making and Monitoring Decisions to Solve Problems
U2. Developing Mathematical Language and Communication
U3. Developing Mathematical Reasoning
Number
N1. Understanding Number and Place Value
N2. Understanding Number Relationships and Methods of Calculation
N3. Solving Numerical Problems

Shape; Space and Measures
S2. Understanding and Using Properties of Position and Movement
S3. Understanding and Using Measures
Handling data
D1. Collating, Representing and Interpreting Data
D2. Understanding and Using Probability

Word Problems		Relevant sections of the National Curriculum Programme of Study									
page	topic	U1	U2	U3	N1	N2	N3	S2	S3	D1	D2
4	Number 1	x	x	x	x	x	x				
5	Money 1	x	x	x	x	x	x				
6	Number 2	x	x	x		x	x				
7	Number 3	x	x	x	x	x	x				
8	Number 4	x	x	x	x		x				
9	Number 5	x	x	x		x	x			x	x
10–11	Review 1	x	x	x	x	x	x				
12	Measures 1	x	x	x		x	x				
13	Length 1	x	x	x	x	x	x		x		
14	Time 1	x	x	x		x	x		x		
15	Money 2	x	x	x	x	x	x				
16	Number 6	x	x	x		x	x				
17	Number 7	x	x	x	x	x	x				
18–19	Review 2	x	x	x	x	x	x				
20	Number 8	x	x	x	x	x	x				
21	Money 3	x	x	x	x	x	x				
22	Number 9	x	x	x	x	x	x				
23	Number 10	x	x	x	x	x	x				
24	Measures 2	x	x	x	x	x	x	x			
25	Review 3	x	x	x	x	x	x				
26	Weight 1	x	x	x	x	x	x		x		
27	Measures 3	x	x	x	x	x	x				
28	Money 4	x	x	x	x	x	x				
29	Number 11	x	x	x		x	x				
30	Number 12	x	x	x	x	x	x				
31	Number 13	x	x	x		x	x				
32–33	Review 4	x	x	x	x	x	x				
34	Number 14	x	x	x	x	x	x				
35	Money 5	x	x	x		x	x				
36	Number 15	x	x	x		x	x				
37	Number 16	x	x	x	x	x	x				
38	Number 17	x	x	x	x	x	x				
39	Number 18	x	x	x	x	x	x				
40–41	Review 5	x	x	x	x	x	x				
42	Capacity 1	x	x	x	x		x		x		
43	Measures 4	x	x	x		x	x				
44	Number 19	x	x	x	x	x	x				
45	Money 6	x	x	x	x	x	x				
46	Number 20	x	x	x	x	x	x				
47	Number 21	x	x	x		x	x				
48	Review 6	x	x	x	x	x	x				

Word Problems and the National Curriculum in Northern Ireland

PROCESSES IN MATHEMATICS
P1. Using Mathematics
P2. Communicating Mathematically
P3. Mathematical Reasoning
SHAPE AND SPACE
S2. Position, Movement and Direction
MEASURES (M)

NUMBER
N1. Understanding Number and Number Notation
N2. Patterns; Relationships; and Sequences
N3. Operations and their Applications
N4. Money
HANDING DATA
D1. Collect, Represent and Interpret Data
D2. Introduction to Probability

Word Problems		Relevant sections of the National Curriculum Programme of Study										
page	topic	P1	P2	P3	N1	N2	N3	N4	M	S2	D1	D2
4	Number 1	x	x	x	x		x					
5	Money 1	x	x	x	x		x	x				
6	Number 2	x	x	x			x					
7	Number 3	x	x	x	x		x					
8	Number 4	x	x	x	x		x					
9	Number 5	x	x	x	x		x				x	x
10–11	**Review 1**	x	x	x	x		x	x	x			
12	Measures 1	x	x	x			x		x			
13	Length 1	x	x	x	x		x		x			
14	Time 1	x	x	x			x		x			
15	Money 2	x	x	x	x		x	x				
16	Number 6	x	x	x		x	x					
17	Number 7	x	x	x	x		x					
18–19	**Review 2**	x	x	x	x		x	x	x			
20	Number 8	x	x	x			x					
21	Money 3	x	x	x	x		x	x				
22	Number 9	x	x	x	x		x					
23	Number 10	x	x	x	x		x					
24	Measures 2	x	x	x	x	x	x		x	x		
25	**Review 3**	x	x	x			x	x	x			
26	Weight 1	x	x	x	x		x		x			
27	Measures 3	x	x	x	x		x		x			
28	Money 4	x	x	x	x		x	x				
29	Number 11	x	x	x			x					
30	Number 12	x	x	x	x		x					
31	Number 13	x	x	x			x					
32–33	**Review 4**	x	x	x	x		x	x	x			
34	Number 14	x	x	x	x		x					
35	Money 5	x	x	x			x	x				
36	Number 15	x	x	x		x	x					
37	Number 16	x	x	x	x	x	x					
38	Number 17	x	x	x	x		x					
39	Number 18	x	x	x	x		x					
40–41	**Review 5**	x	x	x			x	x	x			
42	Capacity 1	x	x	x	x		x		x			
43	Measures 4	x	x	x			x		x			
44	Number 19	x	x	x	x		x					
45	Money 6	x	x	x	x	x	x	x				
46	Number 20	x	x	x	x	x	x					
47	Number 21	x	x	x			x					
48	Review 6	x	x	x	x		x	x	x			

Review problems 3

You may find it helpful to use a calculator.
You must show your working.

Wright's biplane

Concorde

Saturn V

1 Concorde carries 148 passengers and crew across the Atlantic from London to New York and back twice a day.
If it has full capacity on each journey how many people does it carry in one week? **4144**

2 The first powered flight was by Orville Wright in 1903.
Concorde first flew in 1969.
How many years after Orville Wright's flight was this? **66**

3 The first air speed record was set by P. Tissandier in 1909 in a Wright Biplane at 34.03 m.p.h. Concorde flies at 1450 m.p.h.
How many times faster is Concorde than the 1909 record to the nearest whole number? **43**

4 The official air speed record in 2001 was held by a MiG-25. It travelled at 1.455 times the speed of Concorde, 1450 m.p.h.
What was the record in 2001 to the nearest whole number? **2110 mph**

5 In April 1990 Concorde travelled from New York to London in 2 hr 55 min. If it left New York at 19:00 when would it have arrived in London which is 5 hours ahead? **02:55**

6 The take-off weight of Concorde is 185 000 kg. The Saturn V rocket was 16 times as heavy as Concorde at take-off.
What was the weight of the Saturn V rocket at take-off?
2 960 000 kg

7 Concorde has a wing span of 83.33 ft and a length of 203.75 ft.
What are its wing span and length in metres to the nearest hundredth? (1 ft = 0.3048 m) **25.40 m, 62.10 m**

Weight problems 1

percentages;
g/kg to oz/lb;
TU×U;
facts/pv to ÷

1 A new 50p coin weighs 15 grams.
What is the weight of a bag of 50p coins that is worth £4.50? **135 g**

2 A golf ball weighs 45 g. This is 30 times the weight of a pygmy shrew, the world's smallest mammal.
What is the weight of a pygmy shrew? **1.5 g**

3 Lucia weighs out 700 g of flour. This is 20% more than she needs.
How many grams of flour should Lucia have weighed? **560 g**

4 A full jar of salt weighs 750 g.
One gram is about 0.035 oz.
What is the weight of the jar of salt to the nearest oz? **26 oz**

5 A box contains 8 jars of low calorie sweetener. Each jar weighs 35 g.

What is the weight of the 8 jars? **280 g**

6 A packet of sugar weighs 2 kg.

What is the approximate weight of the sugar in lbs?
4.4 lb

7 *I am the sum of the multiples of 3 between 20 and 29.*   What am I?

72

26

Measures problems 3

1 Every second of every day 100 lightning bolts hit the ground somewhere in the world.

How many lightning bolts strike in 10 sec? **1000**

2 Becky is making a skirt. She buys a length of material 0.58 m long. She cuts it into two equal lengths.

What is the length of each piece? **0.29 m**

3 Bryn buys a box of 10 table tennis balls. The box weighs 2.5 grams.
What is the weight of one ball? **0.25 g**

4 Samuel's dad buys a case of 10 bottles of wine that is on special offer at £35.99. Each bottle holds 70 cL of wine.
What is the total capacity of the 10 bottles in litres? **7 L**

5 Andrew's room is cold in the winter. His mum buys two panel heaters. One is 63 cm × 95 cm, the other 50 cm × 75 cm.
What is the difference in area of both sides of the two heaters?
4470 sq cm

6 Alice finds that a golf ball weighs 0.043 kg and a tennis ball weighs 0.057 kg.
She puts both balls on the scales. What is the total weight of both balls in kg? **0.1 kg**

What am I?

26

Money problems 4

❶ Mr and Mrs Ross book a cruise to Australia. It costs them £7479 each. They pay a deposit of £2500.

How much is left to pay? **£12 458**

❷ A set of garden furniture normally costs £1190. In a sale it is reduced by 30%.

NORMAL PRICE
£1199
30% OFF

What is the price of the furniture in the sale? **£833**

❸ Moira's dad has to go to France on business. He buys the case and the briefcase.

£73·50

£26·50

What is the total cost? **£100**

❹ A theatre show has an afternoon and an evening performance every weekday.

On the first day the income from the two performances was £9457 and £12 818.

What was the total income for the day? **£22 275**

❺ Daniel wants to learn to play an electric guitar. He buys one for £79.99. Later he sees the same guitar for sale in another shop for £82.50.

£79·99

£82·50

How much more was the guitar in the other shop? **£2.51**

❻ The TV at Walter's house breaks. His dad buys both the TV and the DVD player.

£650

£350

Altogether how much does he pay? **£1000**

❼

I am between 50 and 150.
I am 2 more than a multiple of 3.
I am 2 more than a multiple of 5.
I am 2 more than a multiple of 7.

What am I?

107

Number problems 11

1 In Brazil in 1990 the band A-Ha was watched by 195 000 people at a concert. In the same year 184 000 saw Paul McCartney in Brazil.

How many more watched A-Ha than Paul McCartney?   **11 000**

2 In Ancient Egypt Rames III built warships to defeat the Sea People. Each warship had 6 oars each side.
How many oars were needed for 40 warships?   **480**

3 The cruise ship *Voyager of the Sea* has 1181 crew and can accommodate 3114 passengers.
How many people are on board when the cruise ship is full?   **4295**

4 China has about 1256 million people. In China in the year 2000 there were 124.21 million children in primary schools and 53.84 million in secondary schools.
How many children attend schools in China?   **178.05 million**

5 On average a human being takes 30 000 breaths in a day.
About how many breaths do you take in one hour?   **1250**

6 In the year 2000 the population of the USA was 228.77 million. In the UK it was 57.19 million.

In 2000, how many more people lived in the USA than in the UK?   **171.58 million**

7
Add 2.5 to me and multiply the answer by 7. You will get 70.

What am I?

7.5

Number problems 12

percentages;
four operations with
large numbers;
−ve numbers

1 In 1997 Heathrow airport had 44 262 000 passengers. London Gatwick had 19 417 000.

How many more passengers did Heathrow have than Gatwick? **24 845 000**

2 Every second of every day 400 Kit-kats are eaten.

What is the total number of Kit-kats eaten in a day? **34 560 000**

---

3 In Verkhoyansk, Siberia the temperature has been as high as 37°C and as low as −68°C.
What is the range of temperature? **105°C**

---

4 North Carolina, a state of the USA, in 1998 had 7 425 183 people. Its neighbour South Carolina had 3 760 181.

How many more lived in North Carolina than in South Carolina? **3 665 002**

---

5 In 1997 a total of 14 250 000 people visited Disneyland Paris.

On average how many people is this each day to the nearest whole number?
39 041

6 When completed in 1934 the Strahov Stadium in Prague held 240 000 spectators.
Wembley Stadium held only 30% as many.
How many people did Wembley hold? **72 000**

7

Divide me by 10 and subtract 3 from the answer. You will get 10.5.

What am I?

135

© REPP. Photocopying this material is not permitted.

Number problems 13

multi-step problems

1 In a Wales v Scotland cricket match, Wales scored 257 and 198 runs in two innings. In their first innings Scotland scored 284.

How many more runs does Scotland need to score to equal Wales's total? **171**

| WALES | 257 | 198 |
| SCOTLAND | 284 | |

2 Phoebe got 29 marks out of 50 in a maths test. The teacher re-marked her paper and this time she was awarded 62%.

How many extra marks did the teacher give Phoebe when she re-marked the questions? **2**

3 A sheet has 5 stamps in each row and 10 in each column. At the start of a day a post office has 50 sheets of stamps. At the end of the day it has $10\frac{1}{2}$ sheets left.

How many stamps did it sell in the day? **1975**

4 Mrs Evans orders 200 copies of a magazine to sell in her shop. The magazines come packed in twelves.

How many packs and how many separate copies will she get? **16 packs and 8 copies**

5 Adrian's mum and dad had a party. They bought 5 cases of wine with 6 bottles per case, 8 cartons of beer with 8 bottles per carton and 10 packs of juice with 10 bottles per pack.

How many bottles did they buy? **194**

6 Refuse collectors usually empty 600 dustbins every weekday. On a Monday it snowed and they only emptied one-quarter of this.

How many did they need to empty in the rest of the week to empty their weekly load? **2850**

7

Subtract me from 10 and add 0.7 to the answer. You will get 4.

What am I?

6.7

31

Review problems 4

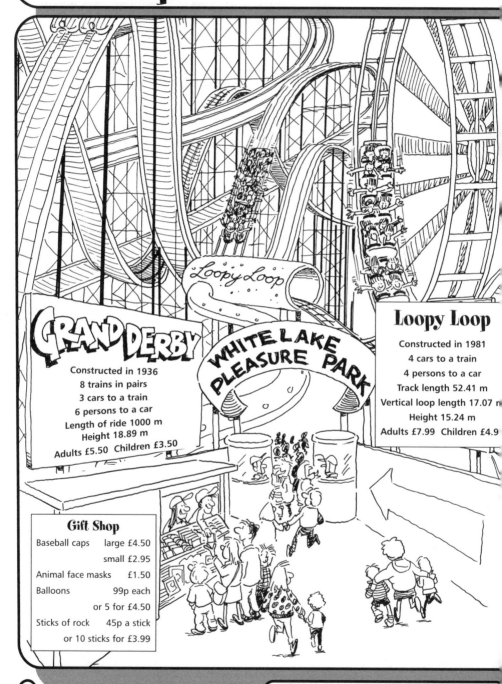

Loopy Loop

Constructed in 1981
4 cars to a train
4 persons to a car
Track length 52.41 m
Vertical loop length 17.07 m
Height 15.24 m
Adults £7.99   Children £4.9

GRAND DERBY

WHITE LAKE PLEASURE PARK

Constructed in 1936
8 trains in pairs
3 cars to a train
6 persons to a car
Length of ride 1000 m
Height 18.89 m
Adults £5.50   Children £3.50

Gift Shop

Baseball caps	large £4.50
	small £2.95
Animal face masks	£1.50
Balloons	99p each
	or 5 for £4.50
Sticks of rock	45p a stick
	or 10 sticks for £3.99

1 The area of Whitelake Pleasure Park is 170 000 m². Of this area, 25% is covered by 150 rides, 35% is shops and cafes and 15% is theatres and cinemas. The rest is parkland and walkways. What area is parkland and walkways? **42 500 m²**

2 When did the Grand Derby celebrate its Golden Jubilee? **1986**

3 How many people are in the eight trains on the Grand Derby when they are all full? **144**

4 Each train is 9.5 metres long. When a pair of trains in the Grand Derby stop at the station the four pairs are equi-distant on the track. What is the distance between the back of one pair of trains and the front of the next? **240.5 m**

5 How many years after the Grand Derby was constructed was the Loopy Loop built? **45 years**

6 What is the length of the track in the Loopy Loop that is not part of the vertical loop? **35.34 m**

7 When the Loopy Loop has 11 adults and 5 children what is the total income? **£112.84**

8 Jamie buys 7 sticks of rock. Later he goes back for 3 more. How much would he have saved had he bought all ten sticks at the same time? **51p**

9 Mr Hastings buys a large baseball cap for himself and three animal face masks and five balloons for his children. Altogether how much does he pay? **£13.95**

10 How many metres higher is the Grand Derby than the Loopy Loop? **£3.65 m**

11 It is planned to build a Vertical Drop ride which will be 72 m. What fraction of the height of the Vertical Drop is an 8 metre lamp post? $\frac{1}{9}$**th**

12 In 1997 Disneyland Paris had 14 250 000 visitors. The Whitelake Pleasure Park had 1 389 000 visitors. How many more visitors did Disneyland Paris have than Whitelake Pleasure Park?
12 861 000

Number problems 14

❶ A trailer can carry 72 bales of hay. A tractor pulls the full trailer nine times from the fields to the barn.

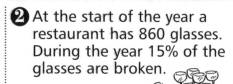

How many bales are taken to the barn? **648**

❷ At the start of the year a restaurant has 860 glasses. During the year 15% of the glasses are broken.

How many glasses are broken? **129**

❸ A container ship carries 4422 containers from Malaysia to England and 3795 from England to Australia.

What is the total number of containers the ship carries on the two journeys? **8217**

❹ It is believed that there are 1537 volcanoes in the world. Some 569 of them are said to be active.

How many volcanoes are dormant (not active)? **968**

❺ In a hairdressing competition each of the seven judges award Julie 9.4 marks out of 10.

What is Julie's total score? **65.8**

❻ A machine makes 1 million chocolates every day. One day, on inspection, it is found that 10 000 of the chocolates are mis-shapen.

What percentage of the chocolates are mis-shapen? **1%**

❼

I am two decimal numbers. The sum of my numbers is 10. The difference between my numbers is 4.4.

What am I?

7.2, 2.8

Money problems 5

+/– decimals;
HTU×TU;
£.p ÷U;
facts/pv to ×/÷

❶ Famjad sends a 120 g letter first class for £0.59 and a 310 g letter second class for £0.87.

What is the total cost of the two letters? **£1.46**

❷ Christina sends 23 letters to New Zealand. Each letter weighs 430 g. The total cost is £72.22.

What is the value of the stamps on each letter? **£3.14**

❸ Mrs Berry has an electrical shop. She orders eight electric irons at £31.95 each. Later she sells all the irons at £34.75 each.

What is the total profit Mrs Berry makes on the eight irons? **£22.40**

❹ A post office has available 8p, 20p, 30p, 37p, 40p, 41p and 45p stamps. Jill buys four stamps to send a 500 g letter first class for £1.58.

Which four stamps does she buy? **40p, 40p, 41p, 37p**

❺ A superstore has 37 Tardis computers in stock. It sells all of them.

What is the total income the shop gets from the sale? **£35 409**

❻ The cost of a 7 day holiday in Eastbourne is £289 per adult and £176 per child. The total cost for the Thomas family is £1571.

How many adults and children are in the Thomas family? **3 adults, 4 children**

❼

I am a decimal number. Double me and add 3.4 to the answer. You will get 20. What am I?

8.3

Number problems 15

double decimals;
+/– large numbers;
facts/pv to +;
HTU ×/÷TU

1 Rob did a dive with a degree of difficulty of 8.7. He did a second dive that had a degree of difficulty double his first.

What is the degree of difficulty of the second dive? **17.4**

2 In Sweden in 1995 there were 1 652 000 children aged 0 to 14 and 1 720 000 people aged 15 to 29.

Altogether how many were 29 or younger? **3 372 000**

3 At a golf driving range each player is given four boxes of balls. One weekend 152 players visit the range.

Altogether how many balls are given to the 152 players? **6080**

4 In ten games a hockey team scores a total of 37 goals.

What is the average number of goals per game? **3.7**

5 In 1900 the population of the world was 1633 million. By 1995 it had risen to 5734 million.

By how many had the population increased from 1900 to 1995? **4101 million**

6 One summer's day a boat on Lake Windermere carried a total of 1218 passengers. On each trip it carried 87 passengers.

How many trips did it make? **14**

7 *I am a decimal number. Add 2.6 to me and double the answer. You will get 11.*

What am I?

2.9

Number problems 16

1 For every person who lives in London there are 25 who live in Hong Kong. The population of London is 7.5 million.
What is the population of Hong Kong? **187.5 million**

2 In 2000 Japan had 126 million people. The population in China was ten times this.

How many people lived in China in the year 2000? **1260 million**

3 The population of Sweden in the year 2000 was 9 million. Eight per cent of the people are over 75 years old.

How many people are 75 or younger? **8 280 000**

4 An aircraft has one cabin attendant for every 40 passengers. A jumbo jet has 560 passengers.
How many cabin attendants will it have? **14**

5 Every day France has 180 000 foreign visitors. This is ten times the number that visit the UK.

How many foreign visitors does the UK have every day? **18 000**

6 Debbie was given the same score on the parallel bars and the horse. Her total for the two events was 17.4.

What was her score on the parallel bars? **8.7**

7

I am half-way between 3.9 and 8.5.

What am I?

6.2

Number problems 17

percentages;
proportion;
+/– 2D numbers;
×/÷100

❶ On a course at an Outward Bound Centre there are 58 boys and 45 girls. How many children are on the course? **103**

❷ Of all the recordings sold 2 in every 3 are CDs. In 2000 in the UK 810 000 recordings were sold. How many were CDs? **540 000**

❸ A car-carrying ship is loaded with 12 different models of car. There are 100 of each model. How many cars are on the ship? **1200**

❹ On a three-masted schooner there are 42 children on a training holiday. Of these, 17 are girls. How many are boys? **25**

❺ An Airbus carries a total of 350 passengers. Of these, 90% travel in Economy Class.

How many are in Economy Class? **315**

❻ There are 28 million golfers in the world. One-hundredth of them play in Scotland.

How many golfers play in Scotland? **280 000**

❼

*I am a prime number.
The sum of my two digits is 14.*

What am I?

59

Number problems 18

proportion;
+/– large numbers;
facts/pv to ×;
×/÷1000

1 The *Royal Envoy* has 522 outside cabins and 189 inside cabins. What is the total number of cabins on the ship? **711**

2 When full there are 2385 passengers and crew on board. There are half as many crew as passengers. How many crew are there? **795**

3 Since its maiden voyage the *Royal Envoy* has made 1000 voyages carrying a total of 1.42 million passengers.
On average how many passengers did it carry on each voyage?
1420

4 On a cruise to the Mediterranean there were 1590 passengers. The restaurant had two sittings for the evening meal and the number of passengers was divided equally between the two. How many passengers were at each sitting? **795**

5 Before the start of a cruise 1000 boxes of wine are taken on board. Each box holds 12 bottles, each bottle holding 70 cL of wine. How many bottles of wine are taken on board? **12000**

6 At one port of call the *Royal Envoy* has to anchor in the harbour. The passengers are taken ashore in small boats. Each small boat holds 70 people.
How many journeys from the ship to shore are needed to carry all the 1594 passengers who wish to go ashore? **23**

7 *I am the difference between two square numbers. The sum of the two square numbers is 85.* What am I?

77

Review problems 5

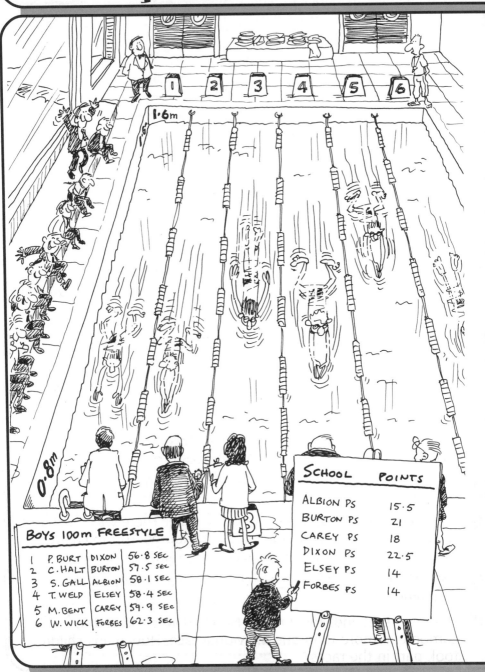

1·6m

0·8m

BOYS 100m FREESTYLE

1	P. BURT	DIXON	56·8 SEC
2	C. HALT	BURTON	57·5 SEC
3	S. GALL	ALBION	58·1 SEC
4	T. WELD	ELSEY	58·4 SEC
5	M. BENT	CAREY	59·9 SEC
6	W. WICK	FORBES	62·3 SEC

SCHOOL	POINTS
ALBION PS	15·5
BURTON PS	21
CAREY PS	18
DIXON PS	22·5
ELSEY PS	14
FORBES PS	14

1 How many schools are taking part in the swimming gala?   **6**

2 The width of the pool is 10.5 metres. The lanes are of equal width. What is the width of a lane?   **1.75 m**

3 The pool is 25 m long and slopes evenly from the shallow to the deep end. What is the depth of the water half-way along the length of the pool?   **1.2 m**

4 How many lengths of the pool did P. Burt swim to win his race? **4**

5 The pool has 315 000 litres of water. It takes 4 hr 22.5 min to fill the pool. What is the average number of litres pumped into the pool each second?   **20 L**

6 Which school is winning the competition?   **Dixon PS**

7 How many points is Forbes PS behind Dixon PS?   **8.5**

8 In each event the winner gets 6 points, the second 5 points, and so on, to the last swimmer who gets 1 point. How many points did M. Bent get in the Boys' 100 Freestyle?   **2**

9 How many events have been shown on the score board?   **5**

10 The result of the Boys' 100 m Freestyle has not yet been entered on the Points Board. Write what the new points will look like when it has been entered.   **19.5, 26, 20, 28.5, 17, 15**

11 How many seconds longer than one minute did W. Wick take to complete the Boys' 100 m Freestyle?   **2.3 sec**

12 By how many seconds did P. Burt win the Boys' 100 m Freestyle?   **0.7 sec**

13 There were 376 people watching the Gala. There was no charge for watching, but every spectator contributed 10p to charity. What is the total amount collected for charity?   **£37.60**

14 75% of the 376 watching are children. How many adults are watching?   **94**

15 There were 20 individual races. No child was allowed to compete in more than one individual race. How many children took part in the races?   **120**

Capacity problems 1

1 Jake buys a goldfish. It is 16 cm long of which 3.5 cm is tail. Jake is advised to put 4 gallons of water into the tank for every 5 cm length of his fish less the length of its tail.

How many gallons of water should Jake put in the tank? **10 gallons**

2 A oil depot has ten storage tanks. Each tank holds 1.5 million litres of oil.

What is the total capacity of the ten tanks? **15 million L**

3 A one litre bottle of apple drink contains 30% pure juice.

How many millilitres of pure juice are in one bottle? **300 mL**

4 Jill's mum fills her car with 10 gallons of petrol.

How many litres is 10 gallons to the nearest tenth of a litre? **45.5 L**

5 Every week the Harris family has a total of 10 baths. They use a total of 175 gallons in the week.

On average how many gallons is used for each bath? **17.5 gallons**

6 Sam uses concentrated orange juice to make a drink. He uses the instructions to make 250 mL.

High juice
Dilute
1 part with
4 parts water

How many millilitres of water does he use? **200 mL**

7 *I am the difference between the smallest and the largest two-digit prime numbers.* What am I?

86

Measures problems 4

1 A new straight road is 100 m in length.
Kerbstones, 92 cm long, are placed
each side of the road.
How many whole kerbstones are needed? **218**

2 On 14th September, 1987 the *New York Times*
newspaper had 1612 pages. It weighed a total of 5.4 kg.
How much did each sheet weigh to the nearest tenth
of a gram? (Remember there are 4 pages to a sheet.) **13.4 g**

3 Pepi II became Pharoah of Egypt in
2246 BC when he was 6 years old.
He died at the age of 102.
In what year did he die? **2150 BC**

4 The river Amazon, in South America, is
6448 km long. The river Nile, in Egypt, is
232 km longer than the Amazon.
What is the length of the Nile? **6680 km**

5 Rachel has a cup that holds 28.4 cL
and a tablespoon that holds 18 mL.
How many tablespoonfuls would
she need to fill the cup? **16**

6 The Caspian Sea, the world's largest lake, is 371 000
sq km in area. The world's second largest lake is
Lake Superior which is 82 414 sq km.
How many sq km larger is the Caspian Sea than
Lake Superior? **288 586 km²**

7

I am a square number.
Both of my digits are even.

What
am I?

64

Number problems 19

1 In the 1996 Olympic Games in Atlanta, USA, there were 10 310 competitors. This was 4225 more than the Montreal Games, in Canada, 30 years earlier.

How many competitors were in the Montreal Olympics? **6085**

2 In 2000 New Zealand had 3.3 million English speakers. Australia had five times as many as New Zealand.

How many English speakers did Australia have in the year 2000? **16.5 million**

3 An actor playing Hamlet in the Shakespeare play *Hamlet* has 1422 lines to memorise.

How many lines would an actor playing Hamlet have said after 1000 performances? **1 422 000**

4 Up to the 1996 Olympic Games the UK had won 395 gold, 215.5 silver and 213 bronze medals.

What is the total number of medals won by the UK? **823.5**

5 In the 1950 soccer World Cup game between Brazil and Spain there were 152 772 spectators. This was 47 082 fewer than watched Brazil play Uruguay.

How many watched Brazil play Uruguay? **199 854**

6 In the year 2000 the population of the UK was 52 million. There are 1433 radios per 1000 people.

How many radios were there in the UK in the year 2000?
74 516 000

7

I am the square of a prime number. The sum of my three digits is 10.

What am I?

361

44

Money problems 6

1 Rachel's mum books a holiday for both of them at Torquay. The cost of the holiday is £299 for her mum and £159 for her.

What is the total cost of the holiday? **£458**

2 The normal price of a Saxon car is £8995. In a sale Mr Cross saves £1365.

What is the percentage saving he made to the nearest whole number? **15%**

3 Mrs Brook went on a cruise to Alaska to see whales, dolphins and glaciers. The cruise cost her £2598 and the executive flight to Vancouver cost £1659.

What was the total cost? **£4257**

4 Mr and Mrs Young took their five children and four more children to see the play *Visiting Grandma*. A child's ticket cost £4.75 and an adult's ticket was twice this.

What did it cost Mr and Mrs Young? **£61.75**

5 Davina saw a digital TV and a DVD player for sale at 'Buy Here' for a total of £1390. Later she saw the same items for sale at 'Rocket TV' for £1199.99

How much cheaper were the items at 'Rocket TV' than at 'Buy Here'? **£190.01**

6 The cost of a wildlife safari holiday is £1398 in January and £1882 in December.

How much less is it in January than in December? **£484**

7 *I am the difference between two square numbers. The two square numbers are between 550 and 650.*

What am I?

49

Number problems 20

halves of decimals;
percentages;
+/− large numbers;
facts/pv to ×/÷

① The island of Cyprus has a population of 650 000. Of these, 78% are Greek Cypriots and 18% are Turkish Cypriots.

How many are Greek Cypriots and how many are Turkish Cypriots? **507 000, 117 000**

② In the year 2000 the *Sun* newspaper sold 3 767 941 copies while the *Mirror* sold 2 321 608.

How many more copies did the *Sun* sell than the *Mirror*? **1 446 333**

③ The estimated population of China for the year 2000 was 1 253 438 000. About one-half of them are females.

What was the estimate of females in China in the year 2000? **626 719 000**

④ In the year 2000 in Russia 7 849 000 children went to primary school and 13 732 000 went to secondary school.

What was the total number of children who went to school in 2000? **21 581 000**

⑤ The number of people in Jamaica is 2.7 million. The number is growing at 2% per annum.

JAMAICA

How many people will be living in Jamaica in one year's time? **2 754 000**

⑥ In a gymnastics competition Marie was awarded 8.3 points by each of two judges and 7.9 by each of three judges.

What was the total score awarded by the five judges? **40.3**

⑦

I am the sum of four consecutive prime numbers. I am between 125 and 140.

What am I?

138

Number problems 21

1 In the first ten overs of a cricket match Robert scored 35 runs. In the next ten overs he scored 47 runs. He then hit 3 fours and 2 sixes in the next over.

How many runs did Robert score in the 21 overs? **106**

2 A block of flats has 315 windows. In a storm 159 of them are broken. The next day workers manage to repair 38 of the windows.

How many windows are unbroken after the repairs? **194**

3 In a tube there are 84 sweets. There are an equal number of seven different colours of sweet. Becky eats five of the red ones.

How many red sweets are left? **7**

4 Five carrying cages each with ten parrots arrived on a plane at Heathrow Airport. The Animal Welfare Officer removed the parrots and put them six to a cage.

How many cages did she need? **9**

5 A shopkeeper got 30 books of 12 first class stamps from the post office. In one week he sells 272 of the stamps.

How many full books and separate stamps has he left? **7 books, 4 stamps**

6 A DIY store had 19 tins of white paint on the shelves. It received a delivery of 50 more tins. All the tins were displayed equally on three shelves.

How many tins of paint were on each shelf? **23**

7 *Add 3 to me and halve the answer. The number you will get has six factors, four of which are 2, 4, 7 and 14.* What am I? **53**

47

Review problems 6

❶ As sound travels more slowly than light we hear thunder 3 seconds later than we see the lightning for every kilometre distance we are away from the centre of the storm.

How far are we away from a storm when thunder is heard 1 minute later than the lightning is seen? **20 km**

---

❷ The Indian Ocean is 10 000 km across at its widest point. It is getting 20 cm wider every year.

How many years will it be before it is 10 001 km across? **5000 years**

❸ The weight of an average African elephant is 6300 kg. The blocks of stone used to build the pyramids were two and a half times the weight of an average African elephant.

What was the weight of a block? **15 750 kg**

---

❹ Every 100 metres up a mountain the temperature drops 0.6°C. Mt Everest is 8850 m above sea level.

If the temperature at sea level is 32°C what is the temperature at the summit of Mt Everest? **−21.1°C**

---

❺ A bottle holds 100 mL of cough medicine.

COUGH SYRUP 100 ml

How many 0.6 cL teaspoons full will the bottle fill? **16**

❻ The surface area of the Earth is 510.07 million km². Rainforests cover about one-tenth of the Earth's surface.

What is the approximate area of rainforest? **51 million km²**

---

❼ The cash price of a car is £5995. How much more does it cost when making a deposit of £99 and 60 monthly payments of £127.66? **£1739.60**